Impressum
Verlag: BABADADA GmbH, Nedderfeld 112 , 22529 Hamburg
Geschäftsführer / Verlagsleitung: Harald Hof
Druck: Books on Demand GmbH, In de Tarpen 42, 22848 Norderstedt

Imprint
Publisher: BABADADA GmbH, Nedderfeld 112 , 22529 Hamburg, Germany
Managing Director / Publishing direction: Harald Hof
Print: Books on Demand GmbH, In de Tarpen 42, 22848 Norderstedt

divide
divide

186/2

classroom
classroom

board
board

school yard
school yard

teacher
teacher

paper
paper

write
write

pen
pen

desk
desk

ruler
ruler

book
book

pupil
pupil

satchel
satchel

pencil case
pencil case

pencil
pencil

pencil sharpener
pencil sharpener

rubber
rubber

drawing pad
drawing pad

drawing

drawing

paintbrush

paintbrush

paint box

paint box

scissors

scissors

glue

glue

exercise book

exercise book

homework

homework

number

number

add

add

subtract

subtract

multiply

multiply

calculate

calculate

letter

letter

alphabet

alphabet

word

word

text
text

read
read

chalk
chalk

lesson
lesson

register
register

exam
exam

certificate
certificate

school uniform
school uniform

education
education

encyclopedia
encyclopedia

university
university

microscope
microscope

map
map

waste-paper basket
paper bin

hotel
hotel

hostel
hostel

bureau de change
bureau de change

car
car

language
language

yes / no
yes / no

Okay
Okay

hello
hello

translator
translator

Thank you
Thank you

how much is...?

how much does ... cost?

I do not understand

I do not understand

problem

problem

Good evening!

Good evening!

Good morning!

Good morning!

Good night!

Good night!

bye bye

bye bye

direction

direction

luggage

luggage

bag

bag

backpack

backpack

guest

guest

room

room

sleeping bag

sleeping bag

tent

tent

tourist information

tourist information

beach

beach

credit card

credit card

breakfast

breakfast

lunch

lunch

dinner

dinner

ticket

ticket

lift

lift

stamp

stamp

border

border

customs

customs

embassy

embassy

visa

visa

passport

passport

aeroplane
aeroplane

ship
ship

fire engine
fire engine

bus
bus

truck
truck

motorboat
motorboat

bike
bike

car
car

ferry

ferry

boat

boat

motorbike

motorbike

police car

police car

racing car

racing car

rental car

rental car

car sharing
car sharing

breakdown truck
breakdown truck

refuse truck
refuse truck

motor
motor

fuel
fuel

petrol station
petrol station

traffic sign
traffic sign

traffic
traffic

traffic jam
traffic jam

car park
car park

train station
train station

tracks
tracks

train
train

tram
tram

carriage
carriage

helicopter

helicopter

airport

airport

tower

tower

passenger

passenger

container

container

carton

carton

cart

cart

basket

basket

take off / land

take off / land

city

city

village

village

city centre

city centre

house

house

city - city

cinema
cinema

advert
advert

street lamp
street light

CINEMA

street
street

taxi
taxi

snack shop
snack shop

pedestrian
pedestrian

pavement
pavement

zebra crossing
zebra crossing

bin
bin

crossing
crossing

traffic lights
traffic lights

hut
hut

flat
flat

train station
train station

town hall
town hall

museum
museum

school
school

city - city

university

university

bank

bank

hospital

hospital

hotel

hotel

pharmacy

pharmacy

office

office

book shop

book shop

shop

shop

florist's

florist's

supermarket

supermarket

market

market

department store

department store

fishmonger's

fishmonger's

shopping centre

shopping centre

harbour

harbour

park
park

bench
bench

bridge
bridge

stairs
stairs

underground
underground

tunnel
tunnel

bus stop
bus stop

bar
bar

restaurant
restaurant

postbox
postbox

street sign
road sign

parking meter
parking meter

zoo
zoo

swimming pool
swimming pool

mosque
mosque

farm

farm

pollution

pollution

graveyard

graveyard

church

church

playground

playground

temple

temple

landscape

landscape

signpost
signpost

way
way

meadow
meadow

stone
stone

tree
tree

hiker
hiker

river
river

grass
grass

flower
flower

valley

valley

hill

hill

lake

lake

forest

forest

desert

desert

volcano

volcano

castle

castle

rainbow

rainbow

mushroom

mushroom

palm tree

palm tree

mosquito

mosquito

fly

fly

ant

ant

bee

bee

spider

spider

beetle

beetle

frog

frog

squirrel

squirrel

hedgehog

hedgehog

hare

hare

owl

owl

bird

bird

swan

swan

boar

boar

deer

deer

moose

moose

dam

dam

wind turbine

wind turbine

solar panel

solar panel

climate

climate

landscape - landscape

waiter
waiter

menu
menu

chair
chair

soup
soup

pizza
pizza

cutlery
cutlery

tablecloth
tablecloth

starter
starter

main course
main course

dessert
dessert

drinks
drinks

food
food

bottle
bottle

fast food

fast food

street food

street food

teapot

teapot

sugar bowl

sugar bowl

portion

portion

espresso machine

espresso machine

high chair

high chair

bill

bill

tray

tray

knife

knife

fork

fork

spoon

spoon

teaspoon

teaspoon

serviette

serviette

glass

glass

plate

plate

soup plate

soup plate

saucer

saucer

sauce

sauce

salt pot

salt cellar

pepper mill

pepper mill

vinegar

vinegar

oil

oil

spices

spices

ketchup

ketchup

mustard

mustard

mayonnaise

mayonnaise

restaurant - restaurant

special offer
special offer

customer
customer

FOR

dairy
dairy

fruit
fruit

trolley
trolley

butcher's
butcher's

baker's
baker's

weigh
weigh

vegetables
vegetables

meat
meat

frozen food
frozen food

cold meat

cold meat

tinned food

tinned food

washing powder

washing powder

sweets

sweets

household products

household products

cleaning products

cleaning products

salesperson

salesperson

till

till

cashier

cashier

shopping list

shopping list

opening hours

opening hours

wallet

wallet

credit card

credit card

bag

bag

plastic bag

plastic bag

water

water

juice

juice

milk

milk

coke

coke

wine

wine

beer

beer

alcohol

alcohol

cocoa

cocoa

tea

tea

coffee

coffee

espresso

espresso

cappuccino

cappuccino

banana

banana

apple

apple

orange

orange

melon

melon

lemon

lemon

carrot

carrot

garlic

garlic

bamboo

bamboo

onion

onion

mushroom

mushroom

nuts

nuts

noodles

noodles

spaghetti

spaghetti

rice

rice

salad

salad

chips

chips

fried potatoes

fried potatoes

pizza

pizza

hamburger

hamburger

sandwich

sandwich

cutlet

cutlet

ham

ham

salami

salami

sausage

sausage

chicken

chicken

roast

roast

fish

fish

porridge oats

porridge oats

muesli

muesli

cornflakes

cornflakes

flour

flour

croissant

croissant

bread roll

bread roll

bread

bread

toast

toast

biscuits

biscuits

butter

butter

curd

curd

cake

cake

egg

egg

fried egg

fried egg

cheese

cheese

ice cream

ice cream

sugar

sugar

honey

honey

jam

jam

chocolate spread

chocolate spread

curry

curry

goat
goat

cow
cow

calf
calf

pig
pig

piglet
piglet

bull
bull

goose

goose

duck

duck

chick

chick

hen

hen

cock

cock

rat

rat

cat

cat

mouse

mouse

ox

ox

dog

dog

doghouse

doghouse

garden hose

garden hose

watering can

watering can

scythe

scythe

plough

plough

sickle

sickle

hoe

hoe

pitchfork

pitchfork

axe

axe

wheelbarrow

wheelbarrow

trough

trough

milk can

milk can

sack

sack

fence

fence

stable

stable

greenhouse

greenhouse

soil

soil

seed

seed

fertilizer

fertilizer

combine harvester

combine harvester

harvest

harvest

harvest

harvest

yams

yams

wheat

wheat

soy

soy

potato

potato

corn

corn

rapeseed

rapeseed

fruit tree

fruit tree

cassava

cassava

cereals

cereals

living room
living room

bathroom
bathroom

kitchen
kitchen

bedroom
bedroom

child's room
child's room

dining room
dining room

floor

floor

wall

wall

ceiling

ceiling

cellar

cellar

sauna

sauna

balcony

balcony

terrace

terrace

pool

pool

lawn mower

lawn mower

sheet

sheet

bedspread

bedspread

bed

bed

broom

broom

bucket

bucket

switch

switch

carpet

carpet

curtain

curtain

table

table

chair

chair

rocking chair

rocking chair

armchair

armchair

book
book

blanket
blanket

decoration
decoration

firewood
firewood

film
film

hi-fi equipment
hi-fi equipment

key
key

newspaper
newspaper

painting
painting

poster
poster

radio
radio

notepad
notepad

hoover
hoover

cactus
cactus

candle
candle

fridge
fridge

microwave oven
microwave oven

kitchen scales
kitchen scales

toaster
toaster

detergent
detergent

oven
oven

freezer
freezer

dishwasher
dishwasher

cooker
cooker

pot
pot

cast-iron pot
cast-iron pot

wok / kadai
wok / kadai

pan
pan

kettle
kettle

steamer

steamer

baking tray

baking tray

crockery

crockery

mug

mug

bowl

bowl

chopsticks

chopsticks

ladle

ladle

spatula

spatula

whisk

whisk

strainer

strainer

sieve

sieve

grater

grater

mortar

mortar

barbecue

barbecue

open fire

open fire

kitchen - kitchen

chopping board

chopping board

rolling pin

rolling pin

corkscrew

corkscrew

can

can

can opener

can opener

pot holder

pot holder

sink

sink

brush

brush

sponge

sponge

blender

blender

deep freezer

deep freezer

baby bottle

baby bottle

tap

tap

heating
heating

shower
shower

towel
towel

shower curtain
shower curtain

bubble bath
bubble bath

bathtub
bathtub

glass
glass

washing machine
washing machine

tap
tap

tiles
tiles

potty
potty

sink
sink

toilet
toilet

squat toilet
squat toilet

bidet
bidet

urinal
urinal

toilet paper
toilet paper

toilet brush
toilet brush

toothbrush

toothbrush

toothpaste

toothpaste

dental floss

dental floss

wash

wash

handheld shower

handheld shower

douche

douche

basin

basin

back brush

back brush

soap

soap

shower gel

shower gel

shampoo

shampoo

flannel

flannel

drain

drain

cream

cream

deodorant

deodorant

mirror
mirror

hand mirror
hand mirror

razor
razor

shaving foam
shaving foam

aftershave
aftershave

comb
comb

brush
brush

hair dryer
hair dryer

hairspray
hairspray

makeup
makeup

lipstick
lipstick

nail varnish
nail varnish

cotton wool
cotton wool

nail scissors
nail scissors

perfume
perfume

washbag

washbag

stool

stool

weighing scale

weighing scale

bathrobe

bathrobe

rubber gloves

rubber gloves

tampon

tampon

sanitary towel

sanitary towel

chemical toilet

chemical toilet

alarm clock
alarm clock

cuddly toy
cuddly toy

toy car
toy car

rattle
rattle

doll's house
doll's house

present
present

balloon
balloon

bed
bed

pram
pram

deck of cards
deck of cards

jigsaw
jigsaw

comic
comic

lego bricks

lego bricks

building blocks

building blocks

action figure

action figure

babygrow

romper suit

frisbee

Frisbee

mobile

mobile

board game

board game

dice

dice

model train set

model train set

dummy

dummy

party

party

picture book

picture book

ball

ball

doll

doll

play

play

sandpit

sandpit

swing

swing

toys

toys

video game console

video game console

tricycle

tricycle

teddy bear

teddy bear

wardrobe

wardrobe

clothing

clothing

socks

socks

stockings

stockings

tights

tights

scarf
scarf

belt
belt

umbrella
umbrella

t-shirt
t-shirt

boots
boots

slippers
slippers

trainers
trainers

sandals

sandals

shoes

shoes

rubber boots

rubber boots

underpants

underpants

bra

bra

vest

vest

body

body

trousers

trousers

jeans

jeans

skirt

skirt

blouse

blouse

shirt

shirt

pullover

pullover

hoodie

hoodie

blazer

blazer

jacket

jacket

coat

coat

raincoat

raincoat

costume

costume

dress

dress

wedding dress

wedding dress

clothing - clothing

suit

suit

nightgown

nightgown

pyjamas

pyjamas

sari

sari

headscarf

headscarf

turban

turban

burqa

burqa

kaftan

kaftan

abaya

abaya

swimsuit

swimsuit

trunks

trunks

shorts

shorts

tracksuit

tracksuit

apron

apron

gloves

gloves

button
button

glasses
glasses

bracelet
bracelet

necklace
necklace

ring
ring

earring
earring

cap
cap

coat hanger
coat hanger

hat
hat

tie
tie

zip
zipper

helmet
helmet

braces
braces

school uniform
school uniform

uniform
uniform

bib

bib

dummy

dummy

nappy

nappy

server
server

filing cabinet
filing cabinet

printer
printer

paper
paper

monitor
monitor

mouse
mouse

desk
desk

folder
folder

keyboard
keyboard

waste-paper basket
paper bin

chair
chair

computer
computer

coffee mug

coffee mug

calculator

calculator

internet

internet

laptop

laptop

letter

letter

message

message

mobile

mobile

network

network

photocopier

photocopier

software

software

telephone

telephone

plug socket

plug socket

fax machine

fax machine

form

form

document

document

buy
buy

pay
pay

trade
trade

money
money

USD

dollar
dollar

EUR

euro
euro

JPY

yen
yen

RUB

rouble
rouble

CHF

Swiss franc
Swiss franc

CNY

renminbi yuan
renminbi yuan

INR

rupee
rupee

cashpoint
cashpoint

bureau de change

bureau de change

gold

gold

silver

silver

oil

oil

energy

energy

price

price

contract

contract

tax

tax

stock

stock

work

work

employee

employee

employer

employer

factory

factory

shop

shop

52   economy - economy

police officer
police officer

fireman
fireman

cook
cook

doctor
doctor

pilot
pilot

gardener
gardener

carpenter
carpenter

seamstress
seamstress

judge
judge

chemist
chemist

actor
actor

bus driver
bus driver

taxi driver
taxi driver

fisherman
fisherman

cleaning lady
cleaning lady

roofer
roofer

waiter
waiter

hunter
hunter

painter
painter

baker
baker

electrician
electrician

builder
builder

engineer
engineer

butcher
butcher

plumber
plumber

postman
postman

occupations - occupations

soldier

soldier

architect

architect

cashier

cashier

florist

florist

hairdresser

hairdresser

conductor

conductor

mechanic

mechanic

captain

captain

dentist

dentist

scientist

scientist

rabbi

rabbi

imam

imam

monk

monk

clergyman

clergyman

tools

hammer
hammer

pliers
pliers

screwdriver
screwdriver

spanner
spanner

torch
torch

digger
digger

toolbox
toolbox

ladder
ladder

saw
saw

nails
nails

drill
drill

repair
repair

shovel
shovel

Damn!
Damn!

dustpan
dustpan

paint pot
paint pot

screws
screws

musical instruments
musical instruments

loudspeaker
loudspeaker

drum kit
drum kit

double bass
double bass

trumpet
trumpet

guitar
guitar

piano

piano

violin

violin

bass

bass

timpani

timpani

drums

drums

keyboard

keyboard

saxophone

saxophone

flute

flute

microphone

microphone

tiger
tiger

entrance
entrance

cage
cage

zebra
zebra

animal feed
animal feed

panda
panda

animals
animals

elephant
elephant

kangaroo
kangaroo

rhino
rhino

gorilla
gorilla

bear
bear

camel

camel

ostrich

ostrich

lion

lion

monkey

monkey

flamingo

flamingo

parrot

parrot

polar bear

polar bear

penguin

penguin

shark

shark

peacock

peacock

snake

snake

crocodile

crocodile

zookeeper

zookeeper

seal

seal

jaguar

jaguar

pony

pony

leopard

leopard

hippo

hippo

giraffe

giraffe

eagle

eagle

boar

boar

fish

fish

turtle

turtle

walrus

walrus

fox

fox

gazelle

gazelle

American football
American football

cycling
cycling

tennis
tennis

basketball
basketball

swimming
swimming

boxing
boxing

ice hockey
ice hockey

football
football

badminton
badminton

athletics
athletics

handball
handball

skiing
skiing

polo
polo

jump
jump

laugh
laugh

hug
hug

sing
sing

walk
walk

pray
pray

kiss
kiss

dream
dream

write
write

draw
draw

show
show

push
push

give
give

take
take

have
have

do
do

be
be

stand
stand

run
run

pull
pull

throw
throw

fall
fall

lie
lie

wait
wait

carry
carry

sit
sit

get dressed
get dressed

sleep
sleep

wake up
wake up

look at

look at

cry

cry

stroke

stroke

comb

comb

talk

talk

understand

understand

ask

ask

listen

listen

drink

drink

eat

eat

tidy up

tidy up

love

love

cook

cook

drive

drive

fly

fly

sail

sail

calculate

calculate

read

read

learn

learn

work

work

marry

marry

sew

sew

brush teeth

brush teeth

kill

kill

smoke

smoke

send

send

activities - activities

grandmother
grandmother

grandfather
grandfather

father
father

mother
mother

baby
baby

daughter
daughter

son
son

guest
guest

aunt
aunt

uncle
uncle

brother
brother

sister
sister

body

forehead
forehead

eye
eye

shoulder
shoulder

finger
finger

face
face

chin
chin

hand
hand

breast
breast

leg
leg

arm
arm

baby
baby

man
man

woman
woman

girl
girl

boy
boy

head
head

back
....
back

belly
....
belly

belly button
....
belly button

toe
....
toe

heel
....
heel

bone
....
bone

hip
....
hip

knee
....
knee

elbow
....
elbow

nose
....
nose

bottom
....
bottom

skin
....
skin

cheek
....
cheek

ear
....
ear

lip
....
lip

mouth

mouth

tooth

tooth

tongue

tongue

brain

brain

heart

heart

muscle

muscle

lung

lung

liver

liver

stomach

stomach

kidneys

kidneys

sex

sex

condom

condom

ovum

ovum

semen

semen

pregnancy

pregnancy

body - body

menstruation

menstruation

vagina

vagina

penis

penis

eyebrow

eyebrow

hair

hair

neck

neck

hospital
hospital

ambulance
ambulance

wheelchair
wheelchair

fracture
fracture

doctor
doctor

emergency room
emergency room

nurse
nurse

emergency
emergency

unconscious
unconscious

pain
pain

injury

injury

bleeding

bleeding

heart attack

heart attack

stroke

stroke

allergy

allergy

cough

cough

fever

fever

flu

flu

diarrhoea

diarrhoea

headache

headache

cancer

cancer

diabetes

diabetes

surgeon

surgeon

scalpel

scalpel

operation

operation

CT

CT

x-ray

x-ray

ultrasound

ultrasound

face mask

face mask

disease

disease

waiting room

waiting room

crutch

crutch

plaster

plaster

bandage

bandage

injection

injection

stethoscope

stethoscope

stretcher

stretcher

clinical thermometer

clinical thermometer

birth

birth

overweight

overweight

hospital - hospital

hearing aid

hearing aid

disinfectant

disinfectant

infection

infection

virus

virus

HIV / AIDS

HIV / AIDS

medicine

medicine

vaccination

vaccination

tablets

tablets

pill

pill

emergency call

emergency call

blood pressure monitor

blood pressure monitor

ill / healthy

sick / healthy

Help!

Help!

alarm

alarm

assault

assault

attack

attack

danger

danger

emergency exit

emergency exit

Fire!

Fire!

fire extinguisher

fire extinguisher

accident

accident

first-aid kit

first-aid kit

SOS

SOS

police

police

Europe

Europe

North America

North America

South America

South America

Africa

Africa

Asia

Asia

Australia

Australia

Atlantic

Atlantic

Pacific

Pacific

Indian Ocean

Indian Ocean

Antarctic Ocean

Antarctic Ocean

Arctic Ocean

Arctic Ocean

North Pole

North Pole

South Pole
South Pole

Antarctica
Antarctica

Earth
Earth

land
land

sea
sea

island
island

nation
nation

state
state

clock face
clock face

hour hand
hour hand

minute hand
minute hand

second hand
second hand

What time is it?
What time is it?

day
day

time
time

now
now

digital watch
digital watch

minute
minute

hour
hour

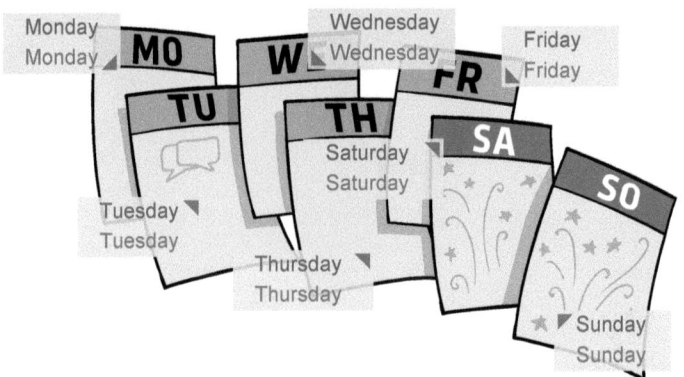

Monday
Monday

Wednesday
Wednesday

Friday
Friday

Tuesday
Tuesday

Saturday
Saturday

Thursday
Thursday

Sunday
Sunday

yesterday

yesterday

today

today

tomorrow

tomorrow

morning

morning

noon

noon

evening

evening

business days

business days

weekend

weekend

rain
rain

wind
wind

snow
snow

spring
spring

autumn
autumn

summer
summer

winter
winter

weather forecast
....
weather forecast

thermometer
....
thermometer

sunshine
....
sunshine

cloud
....
cloud

fog
....
fog

humidity
....
humidity

lightning

lightning

thunder

thunder

storm

storm

hail

hail

monsoon

monsoon

flood

flood

ice

ice

January

January

February

February

March

March

April

April

May

May

June

June

July

July

August

August

September

September

October

October

November

November

December

December

circle

circle

square

square

rectangle

rectangle

triangle

triangle

sphere

sphere

cube

cube

colours

white

white

yellow

yellow

orange

orange

pink

pink

red

red

purple

purple

blue

blue

green

green

brown

brown

grey

grey

black

black

a lot / a little
a lot / a little

angry / calm
angry / calm

beautiful / ugly
beautiful / ugly

beginning / end
beginning / end

big / small
big / small

bright / dark
bright / dark

brother / sister
brother / sister

clean / dirty
clean / dirty

complete / incomplete
complete / incomplete

day / night
day / night

dead / alive
dead / alive

wide / narrow
wide / narrow

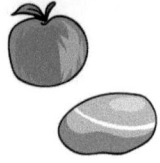

edible / inedible

edible / inedible

evil / kind

evil / nice

excited / bored

excited / bored

fat / thin

fat / thin

first / last

first / last

friend / enemy

friend / enemy

full / empty

full / empty

hard / soft

hard / soft

heavy / light

heavy / light

hunger / thirst

hunger / thirst

ill / healthy

sick / healthy

illegal / legal

illegal / legal

intelligent / stupid

intelligent / stupid

left / right

left / right

near / far

near / far

new / used

new / used

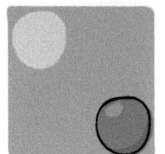

nothing / something

nothing / something

old / young

old / young

on / off

on / off

open / closed

open / closed

quiet / loud

quiet / loud

rich / poor

rich / poor

right / wrong

right / wrong

rough / smooth

rough / smooth

sad / happy

sad / happy

short / long

short / long

slow / fast

slow / fast

wet / dry

wet / dry

warm / cool

warm / cool

war / peace

war / peace

0

zero

zero

1

one

one

2

two

two

3

three

three

4

four

four

5

five

five

6

six

six

7

seven

seven

8

eight

eight

9

nine

nine

10

ten

ten

11

eleven

eleven

12

twelve

twelve

13

thirteen

thirteen

14

fourteen

fourteen

15

fifteen

fifteen

16

sixteen

sixteen

17

seventeen

seventeen

18

eighteen

eighteen

19

nineteen

nineteen

20

twenty

twenty

100

hundred

hundred

1.000

thousand

thousand

1.000.000

million

million

English

English

American English

American English

Chinese Mandarin

Mandarin Chinese

Hindi

Hindi

Spanish

Spanish

French

French

Arabic

Arabic

Russian

Russian

Portuguese

Portuguese

Bengali

Bengali

German

German

Japanese

Japanese

I

I

you

you

he / she / it

he / she / it

we

we

you

you

they

they

who?

who?

what?

what?

how?

how?

where?

where?

when?

when?

name

name

behind

behind

in

in

in front of

in front of

over

over

on

on

under

under

beside

beside

between

between

place

place